# THE ROSE GARDEN

# Shrub Roses

## ELVIN McDONALD

# THE ROSE GARDEN

# Shrub Roses

SMITHMARK

ELVIN McDONALD

This edition published by Smithmark Publishers, a division of U.S. Media Holdings, Inc., 115 West 18th Street, New York, NY 10011.

Smithmark books are available for bulk purchase for sales promotion and premium use. For details, write or call the manager of special sales, Smithmark Publishers, 115 West 18th Street, New York, NY 10011.

TEXT AND PHOTOGRAPHY: Elvin McDonald
DESIGN: Stephen Fay
SERIES EDITOR: Kristen Schilo, Gato & Maui Productions

Printed and bound in Hong Kong

10 9 8 7 6 5 4 3 2 1

ISBN: 0-7651-9066-4

Library of Congress Cataloging-in-Publication Data

McDonald, Elvin.
    Shrub Roses / by Elvin McDonald.
        p. cm. —(Rose garden series)
    ISBN 0-7651-9066-4 (alk. paper)
    1. Roses—varieties. 2. Rose culture. I. Title. II. Series

McDonald. Elvin. Rose garden series.
    SB411.6.M36    1998
    635.9´33734–dc21              98-25862
                                  CIP

DEDICATION

To the memory of Edith Manning, the neighbor who got me started with a 'Harison's Yellow' rose when I was five years old.

*Thanks especially*
*to Carol Hendrick of Brenham, Texas,*
*for helping edit the pictures at the outset,*
*to Hilary Winkler of San Francisco,*
*my research assistant,*
*who helped sort the words at the end,*
*to Dave Kvitne,*
*who actually dug the beds*
*and planted the roses in my garden...*
*and*
*to the gardeners*
*who permitted me to photograph*
*in their gardens...*

*Shrub Roses* and its three sibling books from *The Rose Garden* series, *Climbing Roses, Tea Roses*, and *Old-Fashioned Roses*, have their beginnings in the first rose I planted at age five, about fifty-five years ago, but most specifically in the season (1985) when it was my privilege to work for days and weeks alongside world-class rosarian Stephen Scanniello in the Cranford Rose Garden at the Brooklyn Botanic Garden. Later, I grew and sold roses in Houston, Texas, and I am now in the process of planting my own rose garden in West Des Moines, Iowa. Book teammates, publisher Marta Hallett, series editor Kristen Schilo, and designer Stephen Fay, helped make my *Color Garden* series, *Red, White, Blue*, and *Yellow*, an international success. *The Rose Garden* series is written in the same spirit, to say the big things about a complex subject in a small book.

# Contents

# *Classics*

**IN THE STRICTEST SENSE,** all roses are shrubs. We will concentrate on the more narrowly defined class of shrub roses, as well as some of the various persuasions known for being remarkably carefree. By definition, shrub roses are carefree—the same welcome trait associated with shrubs in general. As it happens, hybrids of hybrid teas and floribundas often turn out to be modern shrub roses. To locate the source of the old shrub roses look to the species and their hybrids, bearing in mind that some have arisen in nature without the help of humankind.

Classics among early shrub and carefree roses are the featured subjects of this chapter. All were in existence before the introduction of 'Bonica' in 1987, the first shrub rose to be honored by All-America Rose Selections (AARS).

Since there are probably thousands from which to choose, the shrub roses pictured in these pages or written about represent only a sampling—admittedly the choice of one passionate rose grower, but these are an indication of some of the most reliable top performers.

**AT LEFT AND RIGHT:** The eglantine or sweet briar, *Rosa eglanteria,* is native to Europe. For its apple-scented leaves alone, it has been cultivated since the beginning of gardens. The spring flowers, on a shrub that can reach 10 feet tall, are abundantly fragrant.

10        *Classics*

Cluster-flowered multiflora and wichuraiana hybrid roses are often ramblers and as such may be thought inappropriate for a small garden or where the annual sorting out of old and new canes, removing the flowered, and tying in the canes for the next flowering, represents too much upkeep. This is entirely unfounded since the hybrid musks belong to *Rosa multiflora* and include such outstanding shrub roses as 'Ballerina,' 'Belinda,' 'Cornelia,' and 'Kathleen.'

The genes of *R. multiflora* have been carried into the modern cluster-flowered rose, first the polyanthas, then, beginning around 1940, into the floribundas. Floribundas were the first group to address a contemporary need for bedding roses that would stay covered in blooms over a long season in return for the least amount of maintenance.

All-time greats among floribunda roses include 'Angel Face' (lavender mauve), 'Apricot Nectar' (orange blend), 'Betty Prior' (carmine-pink, single), 'Europeana' (red, red), 'Fashion' (salmon-coral), 'French Lace' (ivory), 'Iceberg' ("laundry" white), and 'Pinocchio' (pink).

ABOVE: Floribunda 'Stadt Den Helder' (1979), from Dutch breeder Peter Ilsink, will make a splendid hedge to 6 ft. Cold-tolerant, disease-resistant, and everblooming.
AT LEFT: Cluster-flowered multiflora and wichuraiana hybrid roses are well enough behaved for home gardens, yet sturdy enough for planting along a public walkway such as this one in Winchester, England.

**CLOCKWISE FROM LEFT:** Damask 'Ispahan' (Middle East, before 1832) blooms gloriously, to 10 ft., heralding summer with its perfume. 'Sir Walter Raleigh' (David Austin, 1985) has cupped, fragrant blooms above bushy growth, 4-6 ft. 'Frulingsmorgen' (Kordes, 1942), a Scotch rose, has moderate fragrance; large red hips; shrub 5-7 ft.; main flowering: spring. 'Sally Holmes' (Holmes of England, 1976) is a shrub (can be a climber in all but coldest winters). Apricot buds; shrub. 'Golden Wings' (Shepherd, 1956) has light fragrance, vigorous plants (4-8 ft. tall), and is in bloom all season. 'Nevada' (Pedro Dot, 1927) has lots of flowers on short stems in spring; may repeat.

Except for their reliability as carefree shrub roses, the two cultivars pictured here are essentially opposites, one being like a wild or species rose with single or semidouble flowers in a once-yearly flowering, the other a modern, cluster-flowered rose having individually large flowers (hybrid tea) over a long season, from early summer until hard frost in the fall.

'Harison's Yellow,' as it is commonly known, or *Rosa* x *harisonii*, is thought to be the progeny of a cross between *R. pimpinellifolia* by *R. foetida,* made in a New York City backyard and introduced in 1830. Because of the plant system's suckering habit, with underground shoots traveling horizontally and then appearing aboveground at some distance from the parent stock, in terms of early 19th century demand, this is a rose that is easy to share, and relatively easy to propagate. It soon traveled in all directions away from

New York and did so well in the wild west that it came to be known as the "yellow rose of Texas," a misnomer of sorts since the epithet belonged to a beautiful woman, not a flower.

'Harison's Yellow' can be maintained as a specimen, simply by severing any over-extended shoots with a sharpshooter spade. It can also be a marvelous, utterly carefree shrub in a country or cottage garden. But it will never look lovelier than when blue larkspurs have self-sown themselves among its yellow and innocently sweet-smelling roses.

'Gypsy' can be a knockout in the garden, but it also makes a stunning cut flower, creating a bouquet on one stem. Since the canes are naturally vigorous, a tall vase can be instantly filled with long-stemmed roses that will sometimes last longer in water freshened daily than if left on the bush.

**AT LEFT:** 'Harison's Yellow' originated in a New York City backyard in 1830 and is now recognized as one of the hardiest, most widely adapted shrub roses in America. Spring-blooming, 5-8 ft. tall; may spread underground. Strong fragrance; brown-black hips. **AT RIGHT:** 'Gypsy' (1972) has long stems, 5-in., spice-scented flowers, on a bush 2-4 ft. tall.

# Modern

**SINCE THE INTRODUCTION OF 'BONICA,' IN 1987,** there has been a burgeoning interest in hardy, carefree roses. Created by the Meilland family of France, this new type shrub rose was the first such to gain recognition and honors as an All-America Rose Selection.

Also from the Meilland family is 'Carefree Wonder,' which earned its AARS honors in 1991. The pink flowers have a smart creamy white reverse that has the subtly enlivening effect of the right eye shadow. These blooms appear in waves on plants that manage to be both vigorous and compact.

Following the same trend, 'Carefree Delight' took AARS honors in 1996, for its clusters of single roses, mid-pink with a distinctive white eye and a center boss of golden stamens. They appear on arching stems above enduring evergreen leaves, except in rugged places like Minnesota, where the leaves turn bronzy-red. 'Carefree Delight' makes the quintessential specimen, shrub rose, or deployed in formation, serving as hedging and structure to the garden design even in winter.

OPPOSITE: 'Carefree Delight' makes a marvelous hedge or looks divine with blue delphiniums and veronicas.
AT LEFT: 'Carefree Wonder' stands out, with hot pink petals, creamy reverses, and orange hips.

When considering the modern shrub and carefree roses, it is best to remember that in earlier times the present-day companions were relatively uncultivated. Daylilies or hemerocallis, for example, have risen to universal acceptance only since World War II. Hostas, once called funkias, while more associated with shade gardening, often play a starring role in a bed adjoining that of the shrub roses, although they too were little known until the middle of the 20th century.

To achieve a more classical blend of garden types and plant associations, put an old rose such as the apothecary's (*Rosa gallica officinalis*) in the herb garden. This tradition is so old, by now it must be encoded in the DNA of present-day gardeners. Therefore, it is no surprise that modern shrub roses, in particular the single-flowered Carefree and Meidiland cultivars, look refreshingly right in the company of blue-flowered borage, sages, lavenders, rosemarys, veronicas, delphiniums, and agastaches.

Another recent trend in modern shrub and carefree roses is the striping of two or three colors through the petals. This practice recalls the fabled gallica rose, 'Versicolor' or "Rosa Mundi," but with the welcome twist of everblooming habit and disease-resistant foliage.

**AT RIGHT:** 'Pink Meidiland' is thrifty enough to be part of a barrier planting. It is also sophisticated enough to act as a highly rewarding garden shrub—as pictured here at the Hortus nursery and retail garden center in Pasadena, CA, where it is keeping company with the blue-flowered herb borage. The long season of flowering ends in autumn with a lavish display of orange-red hips.

**OPPOSITE, TOP:** 'Carefree Delight' readily takes the form of a shrub in the garden, providing a backdrop for perennials such as daylilies. It provides an exceptionally long and flower-filled season, and strong, disease-free foliage that is evergreen, except in coldest places in winter, where it turns bronzy-red.

**OPPOSITE, BOTTOM:** *Rosa gallica* 'Versicolor,' dating from the 16th century, is ranked as outstanding among the once-flowering shrub roses of old. In its striping, 'Versicolor' is also contemporary, following one of the major trends in rose breeding at the end of the 20th century with flowers striped in two or more colors.

The blended sunset salmon color of 'All That Jazz' (AARS 1992) represents a color breakthrough for modern shrub roses. While it might be too brash for some schemes, it can be conveniently color matched with petunias, bedding geraniums, and everblooming begonias at the garden center. If you believe in the maxim "mass for effect," this can be an expeditious way of getting your deck pots or entry garden to have a pulled-together look without spending too much time or money.

Moreover, 'All That Jazz' resonates with any blue garden flower, such as didiscus, stokesia, delphinium and larkspur, or the usual blue herbs such as lavender, agastache, catmint, and rosemary.

'Lady of the Dawn,' introduced in 1994, is a dreamy shrub rose that grows 3 to 4 ft. tall and has dark green, matte foliage that is remarkably weather- and disease-resistant. The pink-tinged ivory flowers have 10 to 15 petals in ruffly, open formation, and a generous fruity fragrance. It makes a knockout specimen or repeated through a mixed flower border with other whites and pinks, with accents of blue from, for example, delphinium, monkshood, or veronica.

**ABOVE:** Hybrid tea 'Gypsy' (1972) can be more like a disease-resistant shrub. **OPPOSITE. TOP:** 'All That Jazz' won AARS in 1992, a thoroughly modern shrub rose in a blended sunset salmon, and spice scented. **OPPOSITE, BOTTOM:** Shrub 'Lady of the Dawn' (Jackson & Perkins, 1994) shares color subtleties with the great 'Peace.'

**OVERLEAF, LEFT:** 'Carefree Wonder' can be a specimen or a hedge. **RIGHT:** 'Bonica' blooms with extraordinary profusion.

22          *Modern*

## HIP TALK

N OT EVERY *good shrub rose has colorful, long-lasting hips, merely the great ones, for example, 'Bonica,' shown here. They contain the seeds, surrounded by pulp encased in a shiny, leathery skin, in the manner of another rose family member, the apple; a third, the strawberry, forms seeds on the exterior of the fruit, a most unusual habit.*

*Hips vary in size from smaller than a pea to over an inch in length or diameter. The shape can be round, urn, or oval. As they develop, the green hips ripen to some shade of red or orange, ranging from near black to cordovan all the way to a golden apricot.*

*The larger hips, such as those of the rugosas, contain large amounts of vitamin C. If pesticide-free, they can be eaten fresh like an apple, the flesh being surprisingly sweet.*

# Rugosas

**FOR CITY OR COUNTRY, COTTAGE OR CASTLE,** these shrubs from Russia, Japan, China, and Korea are among the hardiest of the rose kingdom. *Rosa rugosa* is variable beyond its recognized varieties 'Alba' (white) and 'Rubra' (red), ranging from clear, dark pink to dark cerise red. It has also been widely used in crossing with other roses, the result being a distinctive class of rugosa hybrids.

The rugosas are famous for their wrinkled or rough-textured leaves that make for a handsome appearance in the garden with or without flowers. They are rarely troubled by blackspot or mildew, but can suffer chlorosis if the soil pH is too alkaline.

Quite simply the rugosas are the most dependable of all shrub roses. They need full

sun and the removal of dead wood in spring. Rugosas can be used to stabilize embankments, in seashore gardens, as informal hedging, and they are said to be spared by deer. Once established, they also tolerate dry soil.

AT RIGHT: 'Thérèse Bugnet' blooms in May-June and repeats periodically. A complex hybrid, it isn't always recognizable as a rugosa.
AT LEFT: The red-flowering form of *Rosa rugosa* is 'Rubra,' brought to the West from Japan in 1796.

26

28      *Rugosas*

Rugosa roses are ideal as framework shrubs, to give the garden structure. They make beautiful backgrounds for low plants and can also serve as windbreaks. Salt-spray tolerance has earned them the names beach rose in America and shore pear in Japan.

Since rugosas are often seen naturalized in sandy dunes near the ocean, it might be assumed that they prefer lean conditions. They will in fact respond to well prepared soil and sound horticultural practices the same as any rose. Good drainage, lots of sun, and adequate air circulation are the requisites. Since sprays damage the leaves, it's fortunate that they are naturally healthy.

Rugosas need little pruning, only the removal in spring of dead and winter-damaged canes. New canes that grow from the base this year will produce next year's flowers. After three years, immediately after the first flush of bloom, remove a third of the oldest canes.

ABOVE: 'Belle Poitevine' (1894, from Bruant of France) is lightly fragrant, repeats, and bears occasional, large, dark red hips. AT LEFT: 'Blanc Double de Coubert' (1892, from Cochet-Cochet of France), was favored by Gertrude Jekyll as the whitest among white roses. Noted for its generous fragrance, recurrent bloom, and outstanding fall foliage, but not many hips.

**CLOCKWISE FROM LEFT:** The 'Rubra' form of *Rosa rugosa* has darker color and more vigorous habit. California breeder Ralph Moore has succeeded in introducing characteristics of the moss rose into his modern, everblooming rugosa hybrids. 'Empress Josephine,' a gallica dating from the beginning of the 19th century, is typical of other rose types that have been crossed with the rugosas, to introduce hybrid vigor and to emphasize desirable traits such as recurrent bloom, fragrance, and handsome, disease-resistant foliage.

AT RIGHT: The red-flowering 'Rubra' variety of *Rosa rugosa* has nearly the same color and circle of yellow stamens as the "French Rose" of antiquity, *Rosa gallica* or *R. rubra*. It blooms constantly, however, instead of once in spring.

AT RIGHT, OPPOSITE: 'Scabrosa' produces an abundance of plump, tomato-red hips.

Not all rugosas are repeat bloomers but many are, delightfully so. The bushes tend to be fairly tall and wide, around 4 to 5 ft., and, with their extra prickliness, they are suitable for forming impenetrable hedging in record time.

There are some rugosas that are excellent ground and steep bank covers. These include three 'Max Graf' cultivars (pink, red, and white), 'Nigel Hawthorne,' 'Lady Duncan,' and 'Charles Alfanel.' It is their natural tendency to grow to 2 ft. tall by as much as 8 ft. wide.

Besides the healthy, wrinkled, mid- to dark green leaves for which they are celebrated, certain rugosas also give exciting fall foliage color, which can be golden, scarlet, or burgundy. Some, outstanding for this effect, are the species, also 'Blanc Double de Coubert,' 'Calocarpa,' 'Carmen,' 'Fimbriata,' 'Jens Munk,' 'Moje Hammarberg,' 'Roseraie de l'Hay,' 'Scabrosa,' 'Schneezwerg,' 'Sir Thomas Lipton,' and 'Will Alderman.'

Rugosa stems are long enough for cutting and make beautiful bouquets alone or mixed with other roses and garden flowers. Only a few blossoms of a highly perfumed rugosa such as 'Hansa,'

'Mrs. Anthony Waterer,' or 'Roseraie de l'Hay' will make a large room smell heavenly.

Rugosas tend to range from white to pale pink to purple-cerise. There is a repeat blooming pale yellow called 'Topaz Jewel.' Not all bear showy, large hips, but many, especially those having single or semidouble flowers are outstanding for fall and winter color.

# *Landscape*

**FASHIONS CHANGE IN THE WORLD OF ROSES** and, as with clothes, cars, or interior design, what is stylish or appropriate relates to all that is contemporary. The energy crisis of the 1970s led individuals and corporations to take a hard look at the high cost of maintenance. Further concerns about the environment made us think of reducing the size of lawns and to stop using poisonous sprays.

Stir into this a nascent consumer awareness movement and the pressing need of rose merchants to adapt so they could profit from this change, and the outcome is the landscape roses of the 1980s, beginning with 'Pink Meidiland' in 1983. From the House of Meilland, home of 'Peace' in the south of France, the concept that roses could be self-reliant shrubs, flowering for long periods, self-cleaning so as not to require dead-heading, and healthy without chemicals, has been widely embraced.

AT LEFT: 'Sevillana' is one of the Meidiland landscape roses. It produces 3-in. double, lipstick-red flowers from late spring until frost, followed by vivid scarlet hips that last through winter. Excellent for a hedge, to 5 ft. tall.

Landscape roses as a class are also the beneficiaries of ever increasing numbers of gardeners who are open to trying plants in new ways. Instead of relegating roses to formal beds framed by clipped boxwood or to climbing on lattice, they welcome the chance to plant appropriate varieties even as carefree, everblooming groundcovers or in island beds with ornamental grasses.

ABOVE: 'Fru Dagmar Hartopp' (1914, German breeder Hastrup) blooms constantly, often most satisfactorily in the fall, at which time there will also be a plentiful supply of the dark red, tomato-shaped hips. Besides fragrance, it is also blessed with vigor, bush form to 3 or 4 ft. tall by a third wider, and dark green leaves of exceptional substance and disease resistance. AT LEFT: One of the most endearing qualities about the rugosa rose is its ability to thrive in urban situations (the photograph was made alongside a busy street in London, England; the yellow and red flowering shrub is broom) as well as sandy dunes near the ocean. The prickly stems can be a barrier hedge.

CLOCKWISE FROM ABOVE: 'Coral Meidiland' grows to 3 ft. tall; blooms profusely in spring and again in fall; outstanding in arid climates. 'Magic Meidiland' is a groundcover to 2 ft. tall by 5 ft. wide with lustrous leaves. Tiny-leaved 'The Fairy' (1932, by Bentall) grows 2 ft. tall by 3 ft. wide and comes into full bloom later than most roses.

40        *Landscape*

In the event a role model had been needed for the modern landscape rose, 'The Fairy' could have served. Introduced by English breeder Ann Bentall in 1932, it was produced from a cross of polyantha 'Paul Crampel' by rambler 'Lady Gay.' Once thought of as a rambler mutation, 'The Fairy' is one of the most loved and widely planted roses. It is said that even if you kill other roses, you can succeed with 'The Fairy.'

In addition to its nonstop clusters of 30 to 40 small double flowers above shiny leaves, its procumbent habit suggests another dimension for 'The Fairy,' that of the tree-form standard. Now this idea has been carried into many of the Meidiland landscape roses, available as 4- or 6-ft. weeping trees.

'Red Fairy' has recently been introduced by California breeder Ralph Moore, with sprays of cherry-red flowers. It can be a bush or standard.

ABOVE: 'Cherry Meidiland' has single, large, cherry-red flowers with white eyes all season, almost hiding the healthy foliage on upright bushes, to 4 ft. tall by half as wide; bright orange hips last all winter. LEFT: 'Autumn Sunblaze' is the ideal nonfading, low-growing, everblooming orange rose, perfect as a specimen, or massed as groundcover (OPPOSITE), to 2 ft. high and wide.

## POTSCAPING

**N**O LANDSCAPE *needed, no latifundium required: Landscape roses will grow perfectly in containers. 'Mystic Meidiland,' for example, has a small, spreading habit to 3 ft. It will grow well and look right in a 12- to 18-in. pot. Use packaged, all-purpose potting soil to fill in around the rose roots. Apply timed-release fertilizer pellets, described on the label as being formulated for roses. Place where there is a half day or more of direct sunlight and water generously. The only thing left for you to do will be to sit back and enjoy the show, maybe invite some friends over. Astound them by revealing the multicolored flowers covering 'Mystic Meidiland' belong to one rose: light copper, yellow hints, blush-pink, creamy white, all at once. Amazing!*

Unlike the rugosas which tend to work better in mixed hedges, the Meidiland landscape roses can also make a beautiful statement when only one kind is used. Recommended cultivars include 'Bonica,' 'Cherry, Coral, Pearl, and Pink Meidiland,' 'Royal Bonica,' and 'Sevillana.'

The groundcovers among the Meidilands include Alba, Fuchsia, Magic, Mystic, Pearl, Red, Scarlet, and White. Planting one color over a sizable area, perhaps a rocky bank, can soon have a dramatic effect. Depending on the variety and how quick you want complete cover, decide on the spacing, usually from 2 to 4 ft.

'White Meidiland,' as an example of a thoroughly modern groundcover, grows to 2 ft. tall by 6 ft. wide and is hardy Zones 4 through 9. It has vigorous, lush, weed-smothering foliage and is ideal for massing.

**AT RIGHT:**
'White Meidiland' (1987) has spreading canes to 5 ft., ideal for snowdrifting an incline. The medium-large flowers have no fragrance but they do have 40 or more petals and glossy, dark green leaves.

# *the Garden*

**DESIGNING FOR LOW MAINTENANCE** is a way to have beautiful roses in all the places you'd like them without taking a lot of upkeep. Among the shrub and carefree types are individuals as well as whole groups with unique possibilities for mixed borders and naturalizing, hedges and hedgerows, barriers and public plantings, and seaside coastal gardens.

The hybrid musks—cold hardiness Zones 5 through 9—are a perfect case in point. Their attributes are such that to say they are repeat flowering fragrant shrubs is no exaggeration. 'Trier,' the first introduced from the Rev. Pemberton's breeding work early in the 20th century, is a repeat climber with sprays of semidouble, creamy white flowers on long, arching growths.

'Ballerina' is multitalented, superb for hedging, and a dream of a low climber for planting under a window. It can also be sited in the garden, where its hydrangea-like pink and white flowers are glorified by the companionship of carpeting pink lamium and the taller white lychnis.

AT LEFT: 'Ballerina' (1937, Bentall) is a hybrid musk with sprays of small, single, pink flowers with white centers that last throughout a long season on an upright, bushy shrub with mid-green foliage. AT RIGHT: The pale delicacy of 'Madame Hardy' stands out against the heroic-sized yew topiary.

ABOVE: 'Honorine de Brabant' or 'Mme. Isaac Pereire' will lace beautifully through lattice fencing. AT RIGHT: 'Buff Beauty,' mid foreground, enhances the distant view.

NEXT PAGE, LEFT TO RIGHT: 'Harison's Yellow' (1830) will grow to one story high in a protected site, as shown here at the Brooklyn Botanic Garden, but to half that height in a windy, arid climate. Masses of small, semidouble flowers appear early in the rose season and make hugely fragrant, if fleeting, prickly-stemmed bouquets for garden effect or cutting.

A particularly valuable attribute of the hybrid musks is their ability to grow in more shade than most roses. Don't expect one to thrive in deep shade where direct sun never reaches, but rather in a place where brief periods of sun and dappled shade strike a balance. It is also true that hybrid musks as a class tend to establish roots in the first season after planting, then really take off and prosper in the second season, much the same as the modern shrub 'Bonica.'

If hybrid musks are never pruned, they will concentrate most flowering in one grand season around the end of spring and the beginning of summer. Cutting the oldest canes back to the base in early spring and shortening all the others will result in an extended season. Cutting for bouquets or deadheading encourages more flowering, but at the expense of showy hips in the fall.

Excellent soil preparation at the outset will help the musk roses give more repeat bloom and also to accept more shade.

*The Garden*

Some shrub and carefree roses are suited to more formal plantings, while others appear more beautiful as casual expressions in a rustic setting.

'Madame Hardy,' that French beauty selected out of the Luxembourg Gardens in 1832 for its white, white flowers smelling of roses but also lemony, is a natural for a formal garden where there is a backdrop of tall, dark green yew hedging and boxwood-edged beds. It will also look elegant in a cottage dooryard garden, in the company of other white flowers or those possessing paler hues of pink, yellow, or blue.

Semidouble or single-flowered roses, whether older versions such as 'Harison's Yellow,' or contemporary renderings like 'Carefree Delight,' can be dressed up or down. They can be exactly what a classic lattice garden setting needs. Conversely, the impression that a rose having single flowers is a gift of nature—pure, simple, wild—these qualities make them ideal for planting around farm buildings, at summer cottages, and country houses. In such settings, they yield wonderful bouquet material.

## SPECIMEN APPEAL: THE BUTTERFLY ROSE

MODERN ROSES, *though known for blooming in several colors at once, have nothing on* Rosa chinensis *'Mutabilis' (early 19th century). The medium to large, single flowers open yellow with coppery orange reverses (the color of the buds), darken to deep pink, then crimson. While roses in general fade with age, it is a trait of the Chinas to darken. The flowers have a silky texture and often appear to have landed atop the bronzy red growth, hence the nickname "butterfly rose." One plant can form a splendid drift accompanied by sage, rue, catmint, stokesia, and lavender.*

Considering the great importance placed on remontancy or everblooming habit in roses during the past century, it is high praise, indeed, when a rose that blooms once a year is chosen to play a prominent role in the garden. The gallicas, with their ability to thrive in poor soil, are a fine example. Bushy shrubs, dense, nearly thornless, they will reward sound horticultural practices with a grand and glorious show at the height of the summer rose season.

So fragrant are the gallicas, after cutting and placing them in a bouquet, glands on the flower stalks leave their perfume on one's hands. Another strong point is that the petals retain the essence of old-fashioned rose even after they are dried. This trait makes them a favorite for making tantalizing potpourri.

Pruning a gallica is a simple matter since it requires removing, at the end of the current bloom season, most of the shoots that have already flowered. This boosts the formation of new shoots for next year's flowers. This once yearly pruning back results in shrubs that are perpetually youthful, vigorous, and not too tall, about 4 feet.

AT LEFT: At Kiftsgate gardens in England, the walk toward a Simon Verity sculpture (framed by pleached, clipped trees) is bordered in summer by deliciously fragrant *Rosa gallica officinalis*, the apothecary's rose.

# *Companions*

**SYNERGISM RESULTS IN A THING BEING MORE** than the sum of its parts, which is precisely what happens when shrub and carefree roses are given flattering, contrasting, or comparable bedmates.

Gertrude Jekyll herself suggested planting 'Old Blush,' the original China rose, with lavender. Since this ancient shrub rose is remarkably disease-free and will prosper in a container, imagine its effect surrounded by English lavender in an 18- to 24-inch earthen pot. Both plants will be flowering and giving off an intoxicating fragrance blend through most of the summer and fall. Together they create a remarkable synergy.

Sometimes it is the simplest color schemes that are the most satisfying. Any garden picture can scarcely be more serene than combining an old-fashioned shrub rose with white flowers such as 'Madame Hardy' or 'Boule de Neige' with sky-blue delphiniums or the long-in-flower and sturdy catmint (nepeta).

**AT LEFT:** 'Ballerina' keeps its place with small companions, geranium, erodium, and pink oxalis at a doorway.

**OPPOSITE:** A shrub rose, dusky, apricot-pink, resembling 'Abraham Darby,' is in dramatic harmony with a reddish purple perennial pea and blue violas.

55

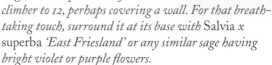

## THE EYES HAVE IT

**T**HERE IS NO *denying that 'Sally Holmes'* (**NEAR RIGHT***) is a beautiful rose that produces large, single flowers in bounteous clusters. Grow it as a large shrub, a pillar to 6 feet, or a climber to 12, perhaps covering a wall. For that breathtaking touch, surround it at its base with* Salvia x superba *'East Friesland' or any similar sage having bright violet or purple flowers.*

*'Ballerina'* (**AT LEFT***) illustrates another way plant combinations can make more out of less. Here the rose is surrounded at its base by a glowing magenta, low-growing species of true, hardy geranium and a white-flowered hebe, both somewhat incidental to the main event: A wall for a backdrop that is nearly covered by a climbing hydrangea, all lacy, white, lime, and green, in fluffy, almost ascending clusters that repeat the habit and overall feeling of the roses.*

*'Bow Bells'* (**AT RIGHT***) has polyantha form that is reminiscent of 'Margo Koster' (salmon-orange) and 'Dick Koster' (dark orange-pink). Here it stands at the top of an old garden wall from which erigeron daisies are spilling, their ray flower reverses repeating the very intense rose-cerise color of the rose.*

*When any shrub or carefree rose is teamed with one or more plants, an object, or a painted structure, you may consult a colorist, but remember to be sure that it is your eyes that are served.*

*If you feel uncertain about a color combination, take a sample of the rose to a nursery or botanical garden and look for the ideal match.*

Hardy perennial flowers having well behaved foliage not given to foliar blights make great companions for shrub and care-free roses. One of the most successful and promising is the penstemon, an American native that has come to be highly respected by the most discriminating gardeners.

The penstemon habit is to form a basal rosette of leaves, above which rises the vertical and essentially self-reliant spike of tubular flowers, reminiscent of snapdragons but less congested, more graceful. The colors are glorious, ranging from whites through pale blues to dark purples and thence a complete range of reds, cool to warm, pale to dark. It is this palette that helps the discerning eye match up the perfect bedmate for almost any shrub rose. As each penstemon spike finishes blooming, deadhead back to healthy foliage. This encourages an extended flowering season.

Compact shrubs of low-growing habit, *Hebe*

**ABOVE:** The spikes of a showy penstemon reach up as though to greet the gracefully arching branches of the rugosa hybrid shrub rose 'Therèse Bugnet,' whose red buds echo the red of the penstemon flowers. This duet begins in early summer and lasts until fall. Minimal deadheading of both rose and penstemon will hurry new buds and help prevent disease.

*albicans* for example, can also be a wise and aesthetically pleasing choice for combining in a garden with a shrub rose. Being evergreen helps make the scene more appealing during the rose's off seasons.

Self-sowing flowers such as opium and Shirley poppies, larkspur, sweet rocket, and purple-leaved perilla can also make charming bedmates for shrub roses, and since they pop up in unexpected places, such volunteers have a way of changing the garden each year so as to keep one's interest keen.

**CLOCKWISE FROM ABOVE:** In early summer, *Rosa gallica* var. *officinalis* takes on new definition with *Hebe albicans*, whose buds are pinkish. 'Kirsten Poulsen,' a 1924 hybrid tea having clusters of single red blooms never stops all season. Here it grows with blue salvias, violas, and bright pink poppies. The buff-pink flowers of 'Grüss an Aachen' appear in profusion until frost; here they are in the company of Shasta daisies next to a redbud tree.

**CLOCKWISE FROM ABOVE:** Clematis 'Jackmani' and the silvery blue 'Perle d'Azur' are heavenly with any rose, especially a pink or buff. As once-blooming shrubs finish, summer lilies can continue the show in harmonious colors. In a border of hot colors, an English rose such as 'Leander' (1982, David Austin), with orange-red buds and orange-apricot flowers, is dramatically enhanced by red poppies, scarlet Maltese cross or lychnis, and a red rose in the background.

It is smart to bed the once-blooming shrub roses with *viticella* clematis such as 'Abundance,' 'Kermesina,' or 'Purpurea Plena Elegans.' Clematis like these are pruned to the ground in early spring. New shoots then grow up through the roses to top out and bloom in late summer. The combination is visually satisfying and doesn't require extra time or knowledge to sort out the parts of the clematis to be cut back.

Oftentimes, it is the flower of the shrub rose that will suggest an appropriate bedmate. A blended color rose, with copper, orange, yellow, and apricot stirred in can be safely accompanied by blues and purples or it can become the catalyst for a more dramatic and daring effect by adding soft to vivid to dark reds. Primarily foliage plants having silver or red leaves can also flatter shrub roses.

The natural form of the shrub rose or how it is trained, such as pegged down to groundcover proportions or spiraled upward on a vertical support, to form a well defined column, helps determine the choice of companion plants. Training roses that are essentially carefree is neither a burden nor a waste of time. It does take patience, but the rewards are a tidier garden with many more rose blossoms. Enjoy!

ABOVE: A tripod helps formalize the shape of 'Rosa Mundi,' *R. gallica versicolor*. Canes are trained spirally around the support, which also yields an abundance of flowering laterals.

# RESOURCES

*Some North American Rosebush Suppliers & Specialists*

**Bridges Roses**
2734 Toney Road
Lawndale, NC 28090
704.538.9412; catalog $1

**W. Atlee Burpee & Co.**
300 Park Ave.
Warminster, PA 18974-0001
800.333.5808; catalog free

**Butner's Old Mill Nursery**
806 South Belt Highway
St. Joseph, MO 64507
816.279.7434; catalog free

**Carroll Gardens, Inc.**
444 East Main Street
P.O. Box 310, Westminster, MD 21158
410.848.5422; catalog $3

**Donovan's Roses**
P.O. Box 37800
Shreveport, LA 71133-7800
318.861.6693; catalog for SASE

**Hardy Roses of the North**
Box 9
Danville, WA 99121-0009
250.442.8442

**Hidden Springs Nursery**
170 Hidden Springs Lane
Cookeville, TN 38501;
catalog $1

**Historical Roses**
1657 West Jackson Street
Painesville, OH 44077
216.357.7270 (SASE for catalog)

**Hortico, Inc.**
723 Robson Rd.
Waterdown, ON L0R 2H1
Canada 905.689.6984;
catalog $3

**Interstate Nurseries**
1706 Morrissey Drive
Bloomington, IL 61704

**Jackson & Perkins Co.**
1 Rose Lane
Medford, OR 97501
1.800.USA.ROSE

**Kelly Nurseries**
410 8th Ave. N.W.
Faribault, MN 55021
507.334.1623

**Louisiana Nursery**
Route 7, Box 43
Opelousas, LA 70570
318.948.3696; catalog $6

**Lowe's Own Root Roses**
6 Sheffield Road
Nashua, NH 03062;
catalog $2

**Mini-Rose Garden**
P.O. Box 203
Cross Hill, SC 29332
864.998.4331

**Moore Sequoia Nursery**
2519 E. Noble
Visalia, CA 83282
209.732.0190; catalog free

**Nor'East Miniature Roses, Inc.**
P.O. Box 307
Rowley, MA 01969
508.948.7964

**Northland Rosarium**
9405 S. Williams Lane
Spokane, WA 99224
E-mail cparton@ior.com

**Park Seed**
Cokesbury Road
Greenwood, SC 29647-0001
864.223.7333

**Pickering Nurseries, Inc.**
670 Kingston Road
Pickering, Ont. L1V 1A6
Canada
905.839.2111; catalog $4

**Plants of the Southwest**
Aqua Fria, Route 6,
Box 11A
Santa Fe, NM 87501;
catalog $3.50

**Rose Acres**
6641 Crystal Boulevard
El Dorado, CA 95623-4804
916.626.1722

**Roseraie at Bayfields, The**
P.O. Box R
Waldoboro, ME 04572
207.832.6330;
narrated video catalog $9

**Roses & Wine**
3528 Montclair Road
Cameron Park, CA 95682
916.677.9722

**Spring Hill Nurseries**
110 W. Elm Street
Tipp City, OH 45371

**Spring Valley Roses**
N7637 330th Street
P.O. Box 7
Spring Valley, WI 54767
715.778.4481

**Wayside Gardens**
1 Garden Lane
Hodges, SC 29695-0001
800.845.1124

**White Flower Farm**
P.O. Box 50
Litchfield, CT 06759-0050
800.503.9624; catalog $4

*Rose Society and Competitions*

**American Rose Society**
P.O. Box 3900
Shreveport, LA 71130-0030
318.938.5402

**All-America Rose Selections, Inc.**
221 N. LaSalle St., Suite 3900
Chicago, IL 60601
312.372.7090

---

### Metric Conversions
APPROXIMATE

| TEMPERATURE | | | | LENGTH | | |
|---|---|---|---|---|---|---|
| WHEN YOU KNOW | MULTIPLY BY | TO FIND | | WHEN YOU KNOW | MULTIPLY BY | TO FIND |
| °F / Fahrenheit temp. | 5/9 (-32) | Celsius temp. / c° | | in. / inches | 2.54 | centimeters / CM |
| °c / Celsius temp. | 9/5 (+32) | Fahrenheit temp. / F° | | ft. / feet | 30 | centimeters / CM |